# *COPYRI(

First off, we want to thank those of you who have legally purchased this material. We poured our hearts and souls into the making of this system and want only those who truly want to get their ex back to have access to these techniques and strategies.

----> If you purchased this material **legally**, then THANK YOU! You can skip the rest of this letter.

We want this material to change your life and we only want the best for you in the future. We also ask kindly that you direct any other people who may be interested in getting their ex back to the Amazon page where you bought this book.

Now that that's over, Let's Proceed....

# Table of contents

# An Introduction (VERY IMPORTANT)

It's okay, break-ups are supposed to hurt. It's natural, expected and healthy to feel pain after a split. Don't get us wrong – it WILL get better. But sometimes things have to get a little worse before they can get better.

If you're reading this, you've just lost someone very special to you. The reasons behind the split are not important right now. What is important is that you are committed to getting them back. Not only do you miss them, but you realize something more – this is the person you're meant to be with.

We know it doesn't always help for someone to say, "I know what you're going through." But look, we know what you're going through. You've most likely heard our story on the sales letter, but we want to reiterate the importance of our very own break-up in relation to what your about to read.

About 2 years ago, we went through a very tough break-up, and as you know, got back together. This book is the culmination of everything we learned and experienced during our break-up and make up. You'll find this book basically broken up into 3 parts: First we are going to go through some "you time" where we give you several strategies to get your head right before we tackle getting your ex back. Next, we will walk through the tactics that will give you the absolute best chance of making up with your ex. And finally, we'll give you advice on how to make your How To Get Your Ex Back last. See? Simple!

Now let's work together to figure our what the heck happened in *your* relationship, and how to fix it up. What can you expect from *How To Get Your Ex Back*? What you CAN'T expect is magic. This takes a positive attitude, time and some hard work.

*Remember* – this book is **not** meant to be lightly skimmed. We're going to work through each chapter together and begin to implement the various strategies
necessary to get your ex back as quickly as possible. This is not a 2-day process, so be patient, and you will be rewarded. Here's the good news: We've done all the hard work for you. Over the course of this book, we'll give you everything you need to get your ex

back. This means time sequences, never-before-used psychological tactics, action steps, and much more.

Read the book, learn from it, and get your better half back in your life.

We're in this together,
Ryan & Kimberly

# 1

# Where's the Love? (Why Your Relationship Ended)

The first thing you think when the love of your life walks out the door is "Why did this happen?" Sometimes the answer is staring at you in the face; other times it takes some soul-searching.

Don't expect to zoom past this chapter – understanding what caused the downfall in your relationship could be the very thing that could save it.  Keep in mind – these tips only apply to couples who were actually in a loving relationship, not one-night stands. You ain't gonna find any "Why They're Not Calling" type-stuff in this book.

## Time To Reflect

Get a pen. Can you write down the reasons behind the split? Maybe you can, maybe you can't. Too often couples part ways without owning up to the full story. Men and women think very differently (do I even have to remind you?), so it can be tough to uncover the truth.

1.
2.
3.
4.

*A note from Kimberly:*

*When Ryan and I broke up, it hurt. I knew in my heart he was the one for me. We told each other how much we loved one another but still parted ways. You see, we both believe marriage is very sacred, and we had to be SURE this was "it." I believed in that decision, and reminded myself every time I wavered.*

Stick with it. Remember, this is IMPORTANT. Think about that person. What do you KNOW about them? What makes them different than anyone else you know? How a person was raised and what they experienced completely impact who they are today.

And chances are, dwelling on this issue can get you to your answer.

You may be thinking... Okay guys, I'm still confused. My ex didn't cheat on me or lie to me – so the reasons aren't quite as clear. Listen, we're gonna give you some insight. Yes, we all may be "different," but we're not that different. Most men, and we're talkin' 80-90%, share very similar wants, needs and desires. Women, same deal. Certain social norms have been instilled in us since we were children that stick with us forever. Let's take a look at some common factors which cause men and women to pack their bags.

> *A Note From Ryan:*
>
> *For me, marriage is a one-time thing. Most people say that, but I really mean it. So when it came time for Kimberly and I to take the next step, we had to be sure. We had been together since we were 18! So I had to take some time as an adult to make sure we were both in this for the long-haul.*

## Why Men Break It Off

Men crave to be respected, to be the provider and protector. If you belittle them, consistently, they check out. Why would they stick around when they "aren't good enough?" And more often than not, they will not cite that as the reason for their departure so as to avoid embarrassment. Men have lots and lots of pride. Dig deep, ladies. Was this an issue in *your* relationship?

And let us give you another little secret… lean in… closer… closer…. MEN ENJOY PASSION! They like to know their partner finds them attractive; enough that their lady love wants to come home to a loving embrace. Ever heard of the 5 Love Languages? 9 out of 10 men would choose physical touch as their Number 1. That doesn't always have to mean sex, mind you.

Remember what it was like when you first got together? Much to their chagrin, you probably took 2 hours to get ready for a date, darn it! You even shaved your legs most of the time. Now, *that's* love. The newness of it all made each day exciting, each date exhilarating.

So here's the bottom line. Barring any special reason why they don't deserve it (cheating, etc.), there's no excuse for not recognizing and acting upon these very innate desires. We'll give it to you straight, if your man doesn't get it from you, he will find it from someone else. You can take that to the bank! Isn't it crazy when you see incredibly beautiful celebrity women being cheated on? Look, men don't leave to find someone more attractive. They leave because they found someone who made them feel more respected or more like a man - even if they have a "Halle Berry" on their arm.

*A Note from Kimberly:*

*Ladies, look, I'll be the first to say how much I LOVE my sweats. And make-up? Ugh. But you know what I love even more? Gettin' sexy for my man. I want him to take me to dinner and feel proud to be standing next to me. Even after 5 years of being together, I make an effort to show him he's worth it.*

What we're NOT saying is for you to spend every waking second praising your man and his studly good looks. But there's gotta be a balance. Sure, you might need to remind him to take the trash out. But you don't need to couple it with nagging remarks to bring him down.

And sometimes they're just scared. Scared of commitment? Maybe. Kimberly's college roommate had her heart broken after a month of blissful dating. She wanted to know why it ended, but he couldn't give a reason - until 3 months later when he came begging for her back. He said he was scared that he found "The One" at such a young age. Well, they're married now (clearly he got over that fear)!

Fighting about every little thing can also be a symptom that something else is wrong. Frustrated men have been known to feel worthless when they see their women constantly upset with them. Nothing they do can make their partner happy. Whether or not they're actually doing right by you isn't the issue – the issue is they'll stop trying, which just leads to more fights.

Re-visit the blank numbered list we provided above and see if you can fill out more reasons for your split.

## Why Women Break It Off

More than anything, women long to feel special. Hopefully this is not news to anyone! Almost all women suffer from some sort of insecurity, and it's up to their partner to help them forget about it.

Again, think about when you two first met. You gave her flowers, didn't you? You took her out for romantic evenings or wrote flirty cards.

We're telling you, you can never stop. Maybe tone down, but never stop. Women of all ages like to know they're appreciated for all the things they do to make your relationship or household run smoothly. Most of the time, it's the littlest things that mean the most to them. A simple "Wow!" when they walk down the stairs on a random Monday morning. Or a special email just to say you're thinking of her.

---

*A note from Ryan:*

*Guys, it's easy for us to sometimes forget to do the "little things." Mainly because we get wrapped up in the day or we think the "I love you" we said last week will hold up. Ain't gonna happen. Your girl will be tempted to get that admiration from someone else, and you definitely don't want that.*

---

Women like to be listened to. They're not always looking for an answer, just a loving ear. They want to know they're important enough to turn off the TV and actually hold a conversation. Look, there are going to be times when the romance isn't crazy-awesome. But that's when the friendship part takes over.

Ignoring her will give her the go-ahead to look for greener pastures almost immediately. The strong ones can hold out while their men treat them like a drinking buddy for years on end. But most will start seeking another man to fill that void within 2-4 years.

Have you found any clarity yet? The reasons are meant to help with those of you still pondering the motivation behind your split. But some of you already know the reason, don't you?

## When Cheating's Involved

Well, that's a whole different ballgame. And a different level of pain. We don't have to tell you that both men and women feel a complete loss of trust after being cheated on. "Why aren't I good enough," they wonder.

We can't say it enough – if a man or woman does not feel appreciated or needed – they will go somewhere else to find it. For example, Char gives & gives to Dan, and would like to feel that he appreciates her and couldn't live without her. Dan gives Char no attention whatsoever, not even a simple "thank you." But Char's a pretty girl, and sparks the interest of a dapper young man where she works. He makes her feel special. Char soon gives in to the flirty co-worker almost on purpose. When confronted by Dan who of course finds out (it's only a matter of time, usually!), Char claims Dan made her do it. "You didn't love me enough! You didn't even care about me!"

Guys & gals, it's NEVER your fault for being cheated on. But again, it can be the symptom that something else is wrong. You just need to figure out if this relationship is worth the fight.

Sometimes the cheater is instantly dismayed over their actions and willing to do whatever to get their partner back. Maybe that's you! Good, we're going to help you do it.

Or maybe you're the one who was cheated on. And after being apologized to, you'd like to give it another chance. Good, we'll give you some tips on how to get past the pain and get on with your relationship.

# Your First Move

Alright, here's a tactic that you cannot afford to forget. Right after your break-up - within the first week or two - your ex is probably thinking you are diving into depression. You might be! But they don't need to know that. The goal is to let them know you agree with their decision, and you wish them well.

So, you write them a letter. Handwritten or email, whatever you think is most appropriate. Apologize if you have things to apologize for, but don't drag on. The letter should be one page at the most. This move will surprise your ex like no other - psychologically triggering them to keep interest in you. You are *NOT* ready to reconcile yet - this is just the beginning. But this is a perfect opening move to show your ex your maturity level.

Important: <u>Do not expect a response from them and don't send any response even if you get one back</u>. Remember that! Don't send the letter and sit waiting for hours on end. If they write back - probably with a "Thank You" - leave it at that. This is not the time to open up communication. You'll get there in the next few weeks, just not right now.

# Chapter 1 Take Aways

**Key Points:**

★ Understanding the reasons behind the split could be the very thing that could save it.

★ The fundamental core of most men centers around their desire to be respected. There's nothing that can turn them off faster than belittling them (nagging, lack of passion, etc).

★ It's always important to remember the first days of being together. It's imperative to keep those feelings fresh to make your relationship exciting.

★ Women long to feel special. It's very simple. Quality time, small romantic gestures, and "I love you's" can go a very long way.

★ When one of you cheats, trust goes out the window. You need to decide as the cheater or the cheated on whether or not this relationship is worth the fight.

## Action Steps:

☐ Make sure to fill out the above "Reasons behind the split" list. Don't rush this... really meditate on why your ex checked out. If you need more space, pull open a Word document and go to town.

☐ Write your ex a letter explaining that you agree with their decision and wish them well. Keep it short and to the point!

## 2

# This Is Good For You (You'll See!)

So you're officially single. You've had the "break-up" talk and you should've sent the "goodbye letter" by now. Either way, you're no longer together. We know, it hurts. You're fragile and feeling weak. That's okay! You're human. We'll be the first to tell you that you aren't going to feel better overnight.

Grieving the loss of someone special is an everyday battle to stay strong and focused. Especially if you want to win that person back (isn't that why you're here?)! But the very last thing you want to do is fall victim to a lonely night and ruin your chances of a reconciliation. This chapter will pull apart why you're feeling incontrollable panic and go over some important do's and don'ts for these next few weeks.

## Don't Panic

Every person in the world has gone through a break-up. Either it's your 3rd grade crush who stops playing with you at recess or it's your lover of 5 years moving on. Take relief in the fact that you're not alone. Everyone experiences heartbreak, and more importantly, everyone gets through it.

The biggest thing is that this person was not only your boyfriend or girlfriend, but your best friend, the person you spent most of your time with, shared laughs with and just felt comfortable around. So, it's natural to feel loss of control and panic because that everyday familiarity has been yanked away from you.

Use this time. Use this precious alone time to regain your independence. Take care of YOU. Sure, it'll be hard to get those thoughts completely out of your brain, but if you keep yourself busy you better believe they'll be squashed out of the picture enough to get yourself in order.

# Time To Initiate "Operation: Yes"

Try this method on for size... We like to call it the **Just Say YES method.** It's actually rather simple - say yes to any and all invitations. It's imperative to keep busy so you don't slip up. The "Just Say Yes" Method is initially not the most enjoyable part of this journey. But it gets easier!

> *A note from Kimberly:*
>
> *After Ryan and I had broken up, I had a mess of a day. I cried incessantly and thought about him without stopping (and there was ice cream involved... lots and lots of ice cream). But that was it. I woke the following morning, washed my face, ran a few miles and met a friend for dinner. I didn't want to fall into the depression mode.*

Take a look below; here are some other very important "do's." Pay attention!

1) Exercise. This is one of the BEST things you can do. Exercising daily, even if just a little walk, will give you some sort of routine, brighten up your emotional outlook, and do great things

for your health (We will get into more detail about this in Chapter 4).

2) Bond with friends. This doesn't mean calling your friend and crying about Mr./Mrs. Wonderful. Talk to them, ask about their lives, laugh with them or go to movies with them, etc.

3) Keep up your other routines. Make sure to watch your hygiene (you'd be surprised). Guys: Keep up with the shaving! We don't want you to look like a bum. Look your best. It will help you feel your best. Girls: Do your hair up all fancy-like! Wear a new outfit! It's imperative to feel good about what you got going on.

4) It's hobby time! Come on, you know there's something you've been meaning to spend more time doing. Photography? Golf? Writing? Hop to it!

5) Do something for others. You'll be tempted to wallow during these first few weeks. The absolute best thing you can do to get yourself off the brain is to get others on the brain. Even if it's cleaning out the probably packed closet of yours and taking the extras down to a shelter.

*A note from Ryan:*

*When Kimberly and I got back together, one of the first things we mentioned was how great the time apart was for us. We both spent much-needed time with friends, exercised every day, and became more sure of what we wanted out of life. It was the best thing we've ever done for our relationship.*

Probably even more important than the "do's" are the "DON'T's" As we mentioned in the first chapter, there are reasons for your split. You don't want to incite any more anger or frustration on their part for not respecting their wishes.

You're more likely to make it worse by saying something you don't mean, bring up an old argument or act out… all of which make him or her become turned off at the thought of getting back together with you. So, how do we stop this?

# The Blacklist Tactic

There are many tactics and techniques you'll learn in this book. This is, by far, one of the most important to follow - so do yourself a favor and read carefully.

Ever heard of putting someone on the "blacklist?" It means they aren't allowed entrance or access. Let's pretend your ex is BLACKLISTED from your life. Which means, DON'T call, text, email, snail mail, Facebook, tweet or Myspace your ex. Any and all of the above means of communication need to stop right away. Aside from your opening letter, you are not to initiate contact at all.

**Psychological Impact:** Here's the theory behind the Blacklist Tactic. We as human beings all want what we can't have. It's human nature! We are going to use this to our full advantage over the next 4+ weeks. Have you ever wanted something someone else had? The answer is YES because it's happened to all of us. With the Blacklist Tactic, we want your ex to really believe that they can no longer have you.

Give your ex complete, uninterrupted space (no texts, remember!) for them to take a breather. You'll

appear mature, calm, collected (even if you aren't) because you've
respected the separation without desperate calls or emails. Stand strong! Incorporating the BLACKLIST TACTIC into your recovery will certainly make you seem more attractive to your ex. Hello out there! Ever heard of the phrase "Absence makes the heart grow fonder?" Trust us, it will.

Listed below are a few other DON'TS that you need to be sure to look through and apply to your break-up recovery.

- ✖ **DON'T** allow yourself to wallow. Looking at pictures of the "happy times" will only make it worse. Short cries are okay, but holing up in your home for days at a time is an absolute no-no.
- ✖ **DON'T** overdo it with alcohol or other addictive substances. While they may give you a quick pick-me-up, they will only leave you in a deeper state of guilt and sadness.
- ✖ **DON'T** act out by being promiscuous or overly mischievous. Chances are, your ex will get wind of your transgressions and be completely

disappointed, which would destroy any chances of getting back together.

Making sense? We know it may seem harsh, but this time is so important for both you and your ex. It gives you space to think, rationalize and more importantly, cool off from feelings of anger or frustration. Because let's face it, the day after a break-up you're more likely to yell "You never have time for me!" instead of "Thank you for working so hard to provide a better life for us."

**Remember:** Handle yourself with class. These tips are not meant to encourage you to snub your ex if you happen to run into each other (work, with friends, at the mall). The best thing to do is to be polite, smile, and give a quick greeting. Of course, your heart will be beating like crazy and you may even have a little hand sweat… but on the outside you'll appear suave and even a bit mysterious.

*A note from Kimberly:*

*During Ryan and I's split, we still lived within 5 minutes of each other. A run-in was bound to happen. In fact, it happened when he was meeting a blind date for lunch! I walked in and my heart flew out of my chest. Our eyes met, so I casually walked over to say hello and meet his date. He later told me how that very moment made him question why he ever let me go.*

You've read through this chapter, and hopefully understand how these tips will help. But let's talk candidly, here. This is obviously not going to be all bubblegum dreams and lollipop rainbows. You will feel hurt. But it's very important to not let yourself sink into depression as you're attempting to reconcile with your ex. Now, this is easier said than done, but you gotta start somewhere. Read below for some ways to avoid moving backward instead of forward.

## 5 Tips To Beat The Blues

- Get an accountability partner. If you feel like you're slipping and might call your ex, you'll want that friend or parent that will be there to talk you down.
- Remember the "**Just Say Yes**" Method? It's imperative that you get out and often.
- Get up in the morning - don't let yourself get sucked into sleeping all day.
- Don't center your life around your ex. They're great, but so are YOU. You have a life to lead, now go live it.
- Don't make rash decisions. You're going through a tough time and the last thing you should do is make a decision you'll regret later.

# Chapter 2 Take Aways

**Key Points:**

★ Feelings of deep loss and sadness are normal. Take comfort in the fact that everyone experiences heartbreak, and more importantly, everyone gets through it.

★ Use this alone time to regain your independence. Think about YOU.

★ The "Just Say Yes" method is an extremely powerful way to overcome the break-up blues. It's imperative to keep busy so you don't get off track.

★ One of the most proven tactics out there is The Blacklist Tactic. It's vital to cut off all communication with your ex to show them you respect the break-up. This will undoubtedly show your ex your maturity and make you appear more attractive to them.

★ Don't allow yourself to wallow, overdo it with alcohol, or be overly promiscuous. These short-term pick-me-ups will do some serious damage on your chances of a reconciliation.

## Action Steps:

☐ Implement the "Just Say Yes" method. Say YES to an invite, or, do the inviting yourself and step out of your comfort zone.

☐ Exercise, bond with friends, keep up your other routines, take on a hobby and do something for others.

☐ Review "Beat The Blues" tips for help through this difficult time.

## 3

# It's Over. Should It Be?

**W**e want you to be happy. We really do. So please read this next chapter very carefully.

Everyone deserves that special someone. The person that makes them smile and feel true happiness. Believe us when we say this will happen for you. Most of you are reading this book because you think your ex is that person.

We sure hope so! But before you continue reading and prepping yourself for the reconciliation, we want to make sure your ex truly is the right person for you.

We'll explore how to look back and come to terms with what exactly came between you and your ex... and whether or not this relationship is worth saving.

## Time To Reflect

In Chapter 1, we looked at some reasons as to why men and women leave each other. Chances are, you and your ex fell into one or more of those categories. Look deeper. Think about those Monday mornings, Saturday evenings, nights out at restaurants, walks through the neighborhood... what were the pitfalls in your relationship?

Especially after a break-up, people are tempted to only remember the bad or only the good. That isn't going to help. We've got to look at both. Only then will you be able to remove those blinders and actually make things happen. Get your pen ready, we're going to explore the good, bad and perhaps the UGLY of your relationship.

**The GOOD**
Aww, love. It's wonderful isn't it? Put on those rose-colored glasses for a second and reminisce. You meet hundreds of people over the course of your life, so what made your ex stand out? The beginning stages

of your relationship are very telling about why you fell in love with this person to begin with.

For example, remember that first kiss? That first long talk about anything and everything? What was it about them that gave you butterflies when he or she came around? This is what we need to achieve (again) with your ex. Just like most couples, you probably grew out of this "honeymoon" stage over time. Instead of working to keep things fresh & fun, life gets in the way and we get lazy.

---

*A note from Ryan:*

*Kimberly and I are very routine-oriented people. As time went on, we settled into a (very) boring life. The romance was sucked right out of our relationship. Time apart helped me remember how incredible we are together – how we couldn't keep our hands of each other when we first met! Rekindling our romance was priority number one.*

---

So let's do this. Take out a pen, and write done the qualities that first attracted you to your ex. What made you fall in love? [Some things to consider:

Personality traits, similar interests, spiritual beliefs, etc.]

_____

_____

_____

_____

_____

_____

_____

_____

_____

## The BAD

Alright, now on to the not-so-fun part. No relationship is perfect, and chances are, neither was yours (we know ours sure wasn't!). Sometimes it's ONE issue that caused a break-up, but more often than not it's a few little issues that pile up over time. It's time to face reality and get to the bottom of the "bad" parts of your relationship. Now, be honest. Try to put those possible feelings of anger behind you.

You know what's coming next, right? Yup, another list. This one is equally as important. We know this sucks, but don't hold back. What problems or issues were present in your relationship? [Some things to consider: Differences of opinion over family, faith, hobbies; lack of physical attraction, infidelity, etc.]

_____

_____

_____

_____

_____

_____

_____

## The UGLY

Maybe you are one of those "big issue" people. Did one of you cheat? Or was there some other sort of betrayal?

As we mentioned in Chapter 1, men and women don't just leave their lover unless there are other factors involved. Look at your relationship: What do you think influenced the slip of trust? If you were cheated on, and would like to forgive your ex, you also need to be able to move past it. If you were the one who cheated, you need to be able to properly explain what caused your slip-up and how you plan on fixing it. Be patient, we'll give you guidance on exactly how to do this in just a bit.

## Break-up Myths

The first few days after a break-up are the hardest. You may feel desperate to get back together with your ex. But why? Not wanting to be lonely and knowing our ex is "The One" are two very different things. That's why it's important to examine why you want to get back together with someone who may have hurt you or the other way around.

Take a look below. Have you been known to utter some or all of these statements?

- "Everything will be different if she'll just give me one more chance."
- "I'll never be happy without her."
- "He was my everything."
- "I'll die without him."

These are just a few statements probably lingering around in your head. While they may seem appropriate now, you'll realize they are not at all true. You are perfectly capable of moving on with your life. The question is, should you do it with or without your ex?

If the above list of reasons are the only ones you have for getting back together with your ex, you need to reconsider your thought process. Here's the cold, hard truth – we're giving it to you straight. You will *not* die without them. You *can* find happiness. And, if he or she was your "everything," you need to take a step back and insert some genuine meaning into your life. YOU ARE IMPORTANT and deserve the best, don't discredit your opportunity for a great future.

## The Next Steps

There was a reason for having you study your relationship so closely. This is not a 2-day process; this is a serious decision and undertaking and we'd like you to be as prepared as possible.

Review the lists of "pros" and "cons" you've made above. Feel free to add or remove items you've written over the next few weeks. We want you to uncover the whole truth and nothing but the truth about you and your ex.

And maybe that truth is… "We never should've broken up in the first place!" Think about it. Did you feel blindsided by this break-up? Perhaps a small fight led to the very rash decision to separate. You and your ex were trotting along your merry way and all of a sudden, a pothole interrupts the flow and one (or both) of you overreact. That's a telltale sign that you need to give this another go.

It's decision time, folks. After reading through this chapter, your heart may be feeling heavy. This is tough stuff, we know. Take some time to figure out what you really want. We want you to be a happy, healthy person – confident in what your future will hold.

Does getting back together with you ex just mean more drama, spite and unhappiness? Maybe you're only sitting through that relationship because you're afraid of being lonely. Nope, that life ain't for you! Look, we're here to get you back together with your ex. But NOT if he or she isn't the right one for you. Think. Meditate. Seek advice from friends. Is this the person you want to be with? Do you want to fight for this?

If you do… GREAT. Let's get this party started, then! We have work to do. Read on, dear friends, read on.

# Chapter 3 Take Aways

## Key Points:

★ You're worth it. You deserve the best. Your ex is lucky to have a person like you fighting for them.

★ It's imperative to look at the GOOD, the BAD and the UGLY of a past relationship - no matter how much it hurts - in order to discover the pitfalls you experienced together.

★ Don't get caught up in the many "break-up myths" out there. You are, in fact, perfectly capable of moving on with your life. The questions is, should you do it with or without your ex.

★ It's time to reflect upon whether or not you'd like to reconcile with your ex. Don't make any rash decisions yet, but it's important to have gone through this thought process.

## Action Steps:

☐ Review the lists of relationship pros and cons above. Add to it if necessary over the course of your reading.

# 4

# Focus On YOU Before You Focus On THEM

It's time to get selfish. It's understandable that this is a trying time for you. And we want to be sympathetic to that. But we also want to encourage you to really use this time. As we've mentioned before, you simply must respect the space between you and your ex for right now as you implement The Blacklist Tactic from Chapter 2. What better time than now do you have to tear the walls down and really examine WHO YOU ARE – emotionally, physically and spiritually. It's an empirical truth that everyone could benefit from little "me" time.

We are an ever-evolving people, so take heart in the fact that while you may not be perfect, neither is anyone else! Even if it wasn't your "fault" for the break-up, remember this break-up is just as much about you as it is about them.

---

*A note from Kimberly:*

*The first thing we tend to do when we break up is point the blame completely on your partner. That's what I wanted to do with Ryan and I! But, after a few weeks I realized there were many things I could stand to do better as well. And so it began: A Kimberly makeover!*

---

We're focusing on YOU in this chapter. So should you. Put some energy and real thought into this. It'll get your mind off the break-up blues, that's for sure! So let's get talking...

## The "Wow Factor" Strategy

This chapter is meant to prepare you for facing your ex... well, so is the entire book! But we mean actually standing face-to-face, armed with a new mentality and healthier outlook. As you might have guessed, we're leading you toward a meeting with your ex.

When you see each other, you'll look and feel different than you did when the fights started and the anger built up. Your ex will see those differences and look upon you with new eyes. This is what we like to call the "Wow Factor" Strategy. What is that supposed to mean? It means when your ex sees you next, all they'll be able to say is "WOW!"

The are essentially 3 areas that we need to focus on in order to achieve the "Wow Factor:" The MIND, BODY and SPIRIT.

## The MIND

It'd be great if we could magically change over night – stop our anger problem or quit with the jealousy – but that isn't gonna happen. So don't be discouraged if you run into some roadblocks when assessing what you can potentially improve on. Take a breath and start again.

This chapter is NOT about changing who you are. It's about making you a better you. We want you to be healthy and confident when the time comes to reconcile with your ex. And we'll tell you right now… "healthy" does NOT mean supermodel skinny or buff like Mr. Universe. "Confident" does NOT mean pompous and bitter. Trust us, if you take our advice you'll be overjoyed at the positive changes in your life.

---

*A note from Ryan:*

*When I first saw Kimberly after 5 months, she was glowing. She looked radiant and happy, carefree and full of life. We discovered that both of us took on some great physical challenges when we were apart that helped us improve mind and body all at the same time (her, boot camp; me, P90X). We were truly our "best" selves, and it showed.*

---

## The BODY

Taking care of your body helps in more ways than meet the eye. Looking good helps you feel good, and visa versa. We want you to keep busy, stay distracted, and get on track for some positive enhancements to your life. This is not a weight-loss product. But we strongly believe taking care of your body has lasting effects.

Look, we know how much you might want to lay around all day, but how does that make you feel?

Horrible, right? You feel sluggish and frustrated with your choices. The same goes with not eating at all! Sometimes you lose your appetite after a tough break-up. But again we ask, what good does that do you? Your health suffers, your energy level suffers, and your outlook on life really suffers.

Let's steer clear of either extreme. Deal?

*A note from Kimberly:*

*The first few months of our break-up, I was living alone. The bad parts set in when I was home alone. I pulled out the _____ (fill in really bad food choice here) and feasted away. I woke up one morning, sick of my low energy level and growing tummy pooch, and joined a local fitness boot camp. It gave me a place to go every day and an incredible workout regimen.*

**Get Your Exercise On**

Exercise is great for you. Tell you something you *don't* know, right?! Everyone knows this simple fact. There isn't a magic diet or pills… nothing is better than good ole-fashioned exercise. Why? Well, it's a lot of science-y talk. But here's what it boils down to: Exercise creates hormones called endorphins.

Endorphins have a great effect on your body and mind. Released by your brain during a cardiovascular workout, they act as a natural painkiller and also make you feel happy and confident. Perfect! That's what we all want.

We won't bore you with much more "technical talk"... so let's get on to the tips and best practices.

You simply must get your heart rate up. Pencil in at least 30-45 minutes of cardiovascular exercise, 5-6 days a week. You don't need a fancy gym or weight system to do this, so NO EXCUSES. Start slow if you're not used to strenuous activity. And always, always warin up first! Here are some fun ways to accomplish this first step:

- ~ Walk or Fast Paced Walk
- ~ Jog / run.
- ~ Bike around the neighborhood or to the grocery store.
- ~ Hike a nearby trail.
- ~ Swim / kayak.
- ~ Rock climbing (one of Ryan's favorite activities)

~ Any sport: basketball, volleyball, tennis, racquetball, soccer, etc.

~ Rollerblade.

Those don't look so hard, do they? A "best practice" that both of us have used is to exercise with friends, a.k.a built-in accountability partners. What better way to stay on track than to have a friend banging on your door for an afternoon run?

One of the hardest things about getting into shape is the accountability factor. It's extremely tough (but possible!) to stay motivated 100% of the time. While you just saw several exercises that you can do for free or on the cheap, some of you may like to stick to a more structured program. Here are a few that we used during our breakup.

1) P90X - Awesome workout for men and women (Ryan used this workout)
2) Ate a clean diet - Check out **Paleo Diet For Beginners by Ryan E. Taylor** - Great book and walks you through the steps to eating clean.

You'll notice a change in your outlook almost immediately. Remember, you're not trying to lose

100 lbs or have muscles exploding out of your chest. Setting realistic goals are great, but what's more important is how this will <u>change your attitude</u> and help you get back together with your ex. Isn't it interesting that doing nothing makes us more tired? Exercising, while tiring mid-workout, ends up giving us energy to do even more. So get on with it already!

Once you fall into a good routine, you can use other exercise options to bulk up your regimen. For example, try out a pilates or yoga class. These are great for meditation and getting a good stretch. You also might want to incorporate a weight program into your routine. Make sure to consult a trainer if you're not sure where to start.

**Eating Healthy**

Here's another no-brainer for you. Good food makes you feel good. Aha! A breakthrough. Yes, you're tempted to order up some fast food and/or feast on sugary foods, but that just leaves you feeling down in the dumps. Remember, the ultimate goal is to get back together with the love of your life! We don't want to get caught in sluggish traps.

**Look And Feel Your Best**

Taking notes? Then you'll remember that looking good and feeling good go hand-in-hand. While we're not looking to turn you into a Barbie or Ken doll, we do want you to feel confident in your appearance. Sprucing up can do wonders for your self-esteem – even the littlest things can give you that extra skip in your step!

Yes, it's what's inside that counts. But enhancing the outside is a fun place to start. Positive changes lead to a positive attitude. You simply must have a positive attitude to win your ex back.

## The SPIRIT

It's important to get to know the real you in this process. Spending some time alone to think, meditate or pray is a good way to get in touch with what you really want out of life. It's imperative that you stay at the top of your game – for the most part. You'll have slips and bouts of sadness here and there, but try to stay on task. You're not the first person to go through this and won't be the last. Which is why we've prepared some good ways to keep your mind above the pain.

Here's the thing you have to know and remember: You are unique. You've reacted to this break-up in a very real way that only you can put your finger on. Let's think about this, what values and qualities make you special? Don't get down on yourself in this whole thing. Tell us – what makes you great?

1)

2)

3)

4)

5)

6)

7)

8)

9)

10)

Don't you dare leave any of those spaces blank! You are one-of-a-kind and deserve to be treated as such. Don't let yourself lose sight of the great things you have to offer your ex. While you may need improvements (don't we all!), you need to be able to recognize your awesome qualities.

## Seeking Help

Sometimes you just can't do it alone. Friends and family are great resources to you, so don't be afraid to let your guard down and spill your heart to them. Fill your schedule with coffee dates, basketball games, bingo nights – whatever it is you do for fun, do it, and bring a friend.

Remember, there is NO shame in meeting with a friend for a beer or a weekly sob fest. Each day gets better. Remind yourself of that. You're moving forward, not backward.

*A note from Ryan:*

*I'll be the first to admit that I'm more of a man's man than anything else. So talking with people who weren't Kimberly about my feelings was kind of foreign to me. I knew that keeping it all in was not the way to do things, so slowly but surely I let some close friends in about what I was going through. To say it helped would be an understatement.*

Another good way to help you with your many emotions is to work through this book with a journal.

Often times these chapters will drum up a lot of memories – good and bad – and it's therapeutic to be able to express what's going on in that heart of yours. No lies, no cover-ups… just you. It might feel weird at first, but it doesn't hurt to try!

# Chapter 4 Take Aways

## Key Points:

★   This chapter has been all about YOU. Take some time to reconnect with yourself.

★   Achieving the "Wow Factor" during your first meeting with your ex can do wonders for a potential reconciliation.

★   We want you to be the best you can possibly be. Healthy in mind, body and spirit and ready to take on the goal: get that special person back in your life.

★   Keep up with your health plan, and make it routine. These are tips for life, not just for the next few months.

## Action Steps:

☐   Begin implementing the "Wow Factor" strategy.

☐   Write down 5 different types of exercises you'd like to do.

☐   Get a good cardiovascular workout at least 5-6 days a week.

☐ Write down your current eating habits. Which foods should you work to cut out of your diet?

☐ Begin implementing a healthy eating plan as described in this chapter.

☐ Amp up your appearance (optional). Take what applies to you and work on as needed.

☐ Fill out the "What Makes you Great?" list

☐ Start a journal (optional)

# 5

# (Safely) Play The Field - Why Dating Others Is An Important Step

Let's begin this chapter with a little review. You and your love have split up. You want them back. You're working hard to discover what it is that led to your break-up and improving who you are as a person.

So, dating around may seem counter-productive to you, right? Listen - you are not necessarily dating around to find love. You already found it! But dating others can do wonders for you and your ex. Here's why:

- It may help you fall even more in love with your ex – making you 100% sure that they are "The One."

- Increase self-confidence. We won't sugar coat this; it feels good to get attention from the opposite sex!

- It shows your ex that you are not completely dependent on them for your happiness (but only if they happen to find out that your dating *on their own* – remember, you're still not in contact with them).

- Dating keeps you busy and away from Friday nights at home.

- Dating can be fun! Who doesn't like to go out for nice dinners every once in awhile?

# Get in the Dating Game

*A note from Kimberly:*

*It took me awhile to feel ready to date. I wasn't dating with the intention to find someone special, but just to get out there and have some fun. I met some great guys and really expanded my horizons. I was 18 when Ryan and I became a couple, so it was interesting to actually "date." Scary, and not always comfortable, but really, really good for me (and us).*

Perhaps it's been awhile since you dated. Maybe even years! That's alright – we'll update you on the latest ways to meet potential dates.

**The Set-Up:**
Your friends and family know you best. So what better people to hook you up for a casual date? Tell them you're ready to get back out there, and to be on the look out for co-workers or friends that would be a good fit for you.

**The Internet:**
Of course you've seen the many internet dating "success story" commercials. EHarmony.com and

Match.com are all great places to start. Simply enter in your basic info and interests, and they'll do the rest for you. Don't be embarrassed - nowadays, online dating is just about as common as anything else. Both of us signed up with online dating services while apart - it is the best and easiest way to meet qualified matches. Note: Make sure to keep certain contact info private to be as safe as possible when online.

**The Bar Scene:**
If you're following our "Just Say Yes" method, you're probably out and about fairly often. Spruce yourself up and hit the town for a chance to meet someone while out with friends. They approach you, you approach them – either way it could turn into a fun conversation and maybe a follow-up date!

**Speed Dating:**
You might not have time to dilly-dally around with this person and that, and if that's the case, speed dating might be for you. Bring a friend and have some fun! You'll get the chance to meet many people in just over an hour. And if you don't find a good match that night, at least you got a few funny stories out of it!

# The 411 on Dating

Dating can be fun and it can be not-so-fun. You may still be dealing with some apprehension about whether or not you can do this. Again, you just have to trust us. The best thing to do is to work slowly – we wouldn't suggest throwing yourself out into the dating world a week after you've split with your ex. Remember, you're not dating to "get back" at your ex. You're doing it for YOU.

> *A note from Ryan:*
>
> *Making the decision to date around was hard for me. I enjoyed how comfortable Kimberly and I were together and frankly I didn't like the idea of starting from scratch with a stranger. But dating other girls made me realize how perfect Kimberly and I were for each other. It truly was a necessary experience.*

The best thing to do is to just go for it. Try one date a week. Try two! You'll know what feels right. The first date with someone else will feel weird – we won't deny that. But it gets easier.

We also caution you to be careful when dating. You're obviously vulnerable and you might be tempted to seek comfort in companionship. Do not let yourself become weakened and make what you may call a "big mistake" later on. But who knows? You may meet someone you really do have a connection with. While that can be exciting and certainly a good distraction, you need to take things slowly.

## Dating Etiquette

*A note from Kimberly:*

*The first date I went on post-Ryan was with a friend I'd known for a year or so. He asked me out, and we went to dinner. We had what I thought was a pretty good night, when I made a dating sin. I started to talk about Love Languages! Whoops. I didn't know how to act on a date as it had been so long. Needless to say that was our first and only date. Oh well!*

Dating may be a foreign concept for you. How do you go on a date with someone when all you want to do is run into the arms of your ex? Well, there are definitely some things you should know. Let's take a look:

- ~ <u>Don't spend your whole date talking about your ex</u>. In fact, there's really no need to talk about your ex at all! While they may be sympathetic, they don't really care about your ex. They care about you! Also, it's rude to bring them up when out with another person.

- ~ <u>Be yourself</u>. Talk about what things interest you, what you do for a living, your family, etc.

- ~ <u>Be honest</u>. The last thing you want to do is to hurt someone by leading them on. It may not be the most comfortable thing to do, but be up front about whether or not you'd like to see them again.

- ~ <u>Be attentive</u>. Ask about the other person and truly get to know them. It's interesting to hear other people's stories and thoughts on various issues.

- ~ <u>Keep calm</u>. Remember, this is just for fun. If you don't have the time of your life, don't worry about it!

- ~ <u>Dress to impress</u>. It's good for you to get dressed up and get all sexy. Live it up! This may be the last time you'll ever be single.

- ~ <u>Be open-minded</u>. You never know, you may end up making a great friend.

## So, You're Dating. Is Your Ex?

There's a very good chance that your ex may also be playing the field. We know that may make you feel like an elephant is sitting on your chest. The best thing to do is to avoid hearing about their dating exploits. Don't go on their Facebook or Myspace profiles – it may even be best to "block" them (a good idea when implementing The Blacklist Tactic). Tell your friends you'd rather not know even they may be dying to tell you.

Keep your distance and go on about your way. Diverting from that plan may jeopardize your reconciliation with your ex. We don't want that, now do we? Just as dating is good for you, dating is good for them. Trust that they will experience the same level of awkwardness and frustration when meeting new people. They'll compare you to every person they date, and that can be a good thing! As time goes on, they'll only remember the good times and the memories you two share. Bingo!

# Chapter 5 Take Aways

**Key Points:**

★ While it may seem counter-productive, dating others is actually a powerful technique in the pre-reconciliation stages. Dating around can increase self-confidence and get you out for some fun.

★ You are not to share or "accidentally" share with your ex if you're dating. But if they do happen to find out, it will show them that you are independent and moving forward.

★ It may have been awhile since you've dated. Here are some great ways to meet people: get set-up by a friend, hit up some popular internet dating websites, try your luck at the bar scene or go speed dating.

★ Have fun with it! While on a date, make sure to keep mum on your ex and try to get to know the person.

★ There's a chance your ex may be dating. But don't worry! They'll compare you to everyone they meet and that can actually be a good thing.

**Action Steps:**

- ☐ As soon as you feel up to it, start putting yourself out there to meet potential dates. Generally, we would suggest waiting at least 3-4 weeks before giving it a go.
- ☐ Make sure you're going out on at least 1 date a week if you feel that you're ready.
- ☐ Set up a free profile on the internet dating websites below. The dating "resume" they'll have you build is a great way to get to the bottom of what you are really looking for in a mate. You can keep all 4 profiles, or narrow it down to the one you prefer.
  - ☐ eHarmony.com
  - ☐ Match.com

# Half Way Point!

You're Half-Way There! Keep It Up...

If you've been following our advice closely, you've begun to see some very positive changes in your life. You're out of panic mode and onto independent mode. We suggest you take at least 1-2 months of time apart from you ex. In our case, we took 2 months apart. But everyone's different! So, the next portion of the book will prepare you for that first meeting with your ex when the time is right.

# 6

# The Master Plan To Get Em' Back

Now here's the deal. Some time has passed, and it's time to explore the idea of reaching out to your ex. Notice we specifically chose the word "explore." Reason being is that just because you've reached this chapter, it does *not* mean you're actually ready for this.

The last thing you want is to reach out to your ex and come across as bitter, desperate or needy. You may still be struggling. And that's okay! But if that's the case, you need to hold off on the communication for at least another 2-4 weeks. The key is to get to the point that while you still love and miss them, you recognize that you can cope being without them. You're moving onward and upward and happy about it. Because look, your ex knows you well – they'll know if you're trying to pull the wool over their eyes.

We're not going to sit and tell you how long you need to wait. We waited 2 months before having any sort of contact with each other. Others wait just 1 month. It's all based on what feels right to you. And here's the test:

- Have your daily bursts of crying stopped?
- Do you smile throughout the day?
- Have you been on at least 2 dates?
- Are you exercising and eating right?
- Do you feel confident in the amazing, unique person that you are?

If the answer to those questions is YES, then we think you're ready. But reaching out to your ex after a period of not communicating at all can be really intimidating. You might be a bundle of nerves! It's okay – that's what we're here for.

# A Chess Match

When preparing for this next section, try to think of it as a chess match. We'll give you the psychological strategies and know-how to keep you in control of the game. By the end of this chapter, you'll feel more than prepared to win back the heart of your ex.

You ready for this? Take a deep breath. You'll need to be poised and prepared for anything that may happen. The goal is to get them to meet you in person. Seeing your face will bring about some very real feelings of nostalgia and excitement, which all work in your favor. Remember the "Wow Factor" strategy? This is where it all comes into play.

## Step 1: The Call

So, you need to make a phone call. Stick to these guidelines, and you'll most likely get a YES.

- Remember, it's just a phone call. You know this person inside and out, so don't be overly anxious. You got this! And make sure to keep it brief.
  - If you find yourself too nervous to make the call, try

pretending that your ex is your sibling or long-time friend.

- Don't jump right into the meeting invitation. Ask about work, family – just a little conversation of 3 minutes or less to get you feeling comfortable.

- The idea is to get them to meet you in person.
  - "Hey I was wondering if you'd like to grab coffee on Thursday."
  - "How are you? It'd be great to catch up. Wanna grab a quick drink on Wednesday around 5?"
  - "Hope things are going great for you! How about we meet for lunch on Saturday?"

- DO NOT, we repeat DO NOT discuss anything serious during this brief phone call. This would be a huge mistake.

- Keep it light and fun! But be genuine – don't fake a laugh or anything.
- To increase chances of them answering, try to call after work hours, but before it gets too late.
- Call 2-3 days before you plan on getting together. This way, you'll have time to settle down and prepare.

**What Happens If ? you get their voicemail.**

Well, this is not ideal. But no worries! Be prepared in case this happens. You'll want to leave a very short and sweet message. The best thing to do is to say something similar to this: "Hi! It's _____. Hope you're doing great! I have some free time after work on Tuesday, wanted to see if you'd like to grab a coffee. Let me know! Talk to you soon."

The idea here is to test interest. You'll sound so upbeat that it will make you seem mysterious and appealing. You are not calling for a big hearty talk or to re-hash old wounds, that will be made clear by your message. If you don't leave a message, it may seem like a mistake or a call made in desperation.

If they call you back – great. Mission accomplished. And if they don't? That's a sign that you need some more time apart. Give it another 1-2 weeks before you try calling again.

**What happens if ? your ex says NO to a meeting.**
Don't freak out. Don't beg and plead. Just stay calm. If your ex sounds a bit apprehensive, that's okay. They're just trying to make the right decision. If they do stutter or pause… it's best to hit 'em with a laugh and say something like "It's just a quick lunch!"

They might go ahead and agree to meet you. Good. Jump into the next step. But if they do stick with their "No," then politely accept their decision. End the conversation with "Alright, no worries! Hope you have a great week/weekend. Bye!" See? It sounds like it doesn't even matter to you (although it probably does). But they don't need to know that.

Once you hang up, it's time to lay low for a bit. Try again in a few weeks. If you were the one who hurt your ex, they might still need more space. Give them that space! If they end up calling *you* back, move on to Step 2!

## Step 2: Prepare for the "Date"

Get excited! You should be – you're one step closer to getting your love back into your arms. But the fat lady hasn't sung yet; you've still got some prep work to do to make sure you take full advantage of this opportunity. Here are some tips:

- ✓ **DO**: Take a breather and meditate on what you want to happen. RELAX! You'll be fine. The worst thing you can do is get worked up and nervous. You won't be yourself, and your ex will notice. You don't want things to get awkward.

- ✓ **DO**: Smile, laugh, and smile some more. Remember, the less pressure you put on your ex about this being a "serious" talk, the better. Tell a funny story about work or a friend – just be upbeat. This makes your ex think all sorts of things… "Wow, she's looking great…. It seems like he's changed… She's so mature…."

- ✓ **DO**: Get sexified! Now is the time to shine. Put some effort into your appearance and make sure to spray on a sweet burst of your cologne or perfume.

✗ **DON'T**: Get serious. Not on this date. You may be tempted to get angry or upset over past memories while looking at them – but resist that urge! We're telling you, this is the best thing for you both at this time.

✗ **DON'T**: Spend too much time with your ex – one hour at the maximum! Look at your watch or phone with a casual "Oh gosh, I've got to run…" You'll leave your ex wanting more. PERFECT!

✗ **DON'T**: Ask them if they've been dating. Or if they've missed you. Or if they still love you. Bad, bad and bad.

## Step 3: The Flashback Maneuver

Now we've got an insider's secret for you. It never fails… it even worked on us! As much as you want to appear mysterious to your ex, you also want to do something to remind them how you were when you were together.

It's easier than you think. What sort of thing do you only do with someone you're really comfortable with? Maybe it's call them "babe," or slightly touch their lower back, wipe an eyelash off their face, things like that. This will instantly send a signal to their subconscious that reminds them of when times were great.

That feeling of … Awwwww.

---

*A note from Ryan:*

*The first time Kimberly and I saw each other, we immediately began joking around and catching up on family, friends, jobs, etc. Then out of nowhere, she laughed and said "Babe you're funny…" and we didn't miss a beat. At first I didn't even realize what she had done – all I thought was how cute she was and how natural it felt to be together.*

---

Warning, you need to wait until it feels right. Don't walk up to them and run your fingers through their hair or yell "Hey baby!" You'll get them running for the hills. It needs to feel natural, almost like you did it out of habit. Another telltale sign is how they react to the Flashback Maneuver. If they give you a weird look or verbally react, you need to slow things down a bit.

## Step 4: Ending the Date

Remember, this is not supposed to be a marathon date. You know it needs to be short, great… but how in the world do you end this thing?

You want to leave on a good note. Bow out when things are going really well… which leaves them wanting more as we've already discussed. You'll want to make it appear as if your on your merry way, like you're not concerned about setting up another date. Try to convey an "I don't need you in my life to be happy" kind of attitude.

You need only to react to what they do or say as you make your graceful exit. _You should NOT schedule another date at this time._ The ball is in their court right now, wait and see what they do.

**What happens if? ---> they ask to see you again.**
Go for it! But don't look too eager. The more mysterious you seem, the better. Agree to a date a couple days out so you give them time to miss you and wonder if you really have moved on. You can

even say you'll need to first check your schedule to make sure you're free (SUCH a great move!)

**What happens if ? ---> they try and make a "move."**
While that may be exactly what you're looking for, remember that you're not trying to get them into bed. You're trying to make it last. If you jump right back into things together, they're more likely to take advantage of the fact that they can break up with you and get you right back when they want. DON'T engage. Just make your exit and make plans for a few days out.

**What happens if ? ---> they bring up the past.**
That's fine. It's not the end of the world. Chances are they're looking for an apology or to see if you'll engage in an argument. Don't take the bait. Let them say what they need to say, it might make them feel better to air out their pent-up apprehensions. When they are done, respond with something like "I care very much about the things you have to say. And I do want to discuss them. But let's not do it right now. I just want to catch up with you and have some fun."

## Step 5: The 2nd, 3rd, and 4th+ Dates

You've been doing SO great with this, and you do not want to make a mistake. After your first date, they're just in awe of how different and great you looked and sounded. In most cases, they're just itching for another chance to see you and talk to you and maybe… kiss you?

*A note from Kimberly:*

*After Ryan and I's first "get-together," I was panicked. I thought, okay well where do we go from here? Will he call me? What is he thinking right now? How awful would it have been if I actually asked <u>him</u> those questions! That would've probably scared both of us out of a reconciliation. So, I just sat back and relaxed. Sure enough, 2 days later Ryan called, asking to see me. I kept it simple and didn't rush – that helped us ease back into a relationship so much better.*

So, here's what you do. If you two didn't set up another time to get together, don't worry. Heck, they might even call you to make plans! But if on the off-chance they don't you should wait at least another 4-7 days, depending on how the last meeting went.

Scroll back to Step 1 to practice the same technique you did on the first call. Quick and upbeat!

But this time when you're making the plans, you can crank the date up a notch. And by "crank up," we don't mean to scatter rose petals and put on some Michael Bublé. That's a bit too "coupley." At this point, it's safe to go for a dinner date. Try a new place that the two of you have never been before. Don't limit your time unless you feel the date turning sour. Go and enjoy yourself. Still try to steer clear of emotional arguments – remember you two are supposed to be getting back to the Honeymoon stage where everything is just peachy keen. This isn't meant to avoid conflict altogether; this is meant to simply build back a foundation with your ex before you tackle big issues.

The 3rd & 4th+ dates should be even *more* cranked up. The biggest thing here is to do something completely new and fun. This way, your ex will feel connected to you by way of a shared experience. Some good examples would be going to a baseball game, taking a gondola ride, betting on horses at the track – anything of that nature. Google "fun things to do in…" and insert your city. Some great ideas will pop up for you to consider.

## Getting Intimate

- Men: Your lady will most likely not pounce back into bed with you. Chances are she wants to make sure you are sincere in your intentions. Sex is such an emotional experience for a woman that she may want to wait until she feels completely comfortable with renewing that part of your relationship. Do NOT pressure her. She'll appreciate the respect.

- Women: You are way to important to fool around with someone who isn't committed in any way, shape or form to you. If your ex tries to make a premature move, simply reply that you aren't a fan of "casual sex" and you'd like to wait until you further explore what you two have goin' on. Then again, maybe the two of you are ready! I'm sure your man will no doubt reciprocate. But be careful not to be "used," ladies.

### *What happens if? ---> one of the dates went all wrong.*

First off, don't freak out. You two have been apart for some time, and it may take some getting used to. The best thing to do is to keep up with your routines. Spend some time meditating and just relax. Keep up with the good eating and exercising. Wait at least 1 week, and try calling to set up another date (Step 1). Get back in the game!

### *What happens if? ---> my ex is not reciprocating.*

If you've been the only one to call or show any type of excitement or emotion surrounding your get-togethers, you need to re-evaluate. Sometimes they may just be taking it slowly. Other times, they just plain might not be into it, and don't want to hurt you again by telling you so. Be on your guard for both situations. Remember, you are important and deserve the best.

### *What happens if? ---> if just feels weird.*

Well, the fact that you even are willing to admit that means your love for them has subsided a bit. If you aren't crazy passionate about getting this person back in your life, then HEY! maybe they aren't "The One." Your time apart may have actually changed you in ways you didn't see until your ex was in front of you. Love is hard work, but it's not begrudgingly hard. You work with love, not annoyance. If you see yourself in the latter position, then… well, you know what's coming next. Take a bit of time to really be sure of your feelings, and approach them with your decision.

## Step 6: Make it More

After you've been casually or not-so-casually dating for a month or two, it's time to figure out where you two are at. We know that seems daunting because you don't want to pressure the situation. But, you do need to have an official conversation to ensure you're both on the same page. Chances are this talk of commitment will not happen unless you two have worked out the issues which caused you to break up in the first place. Thus, we need to discuss how to approach those "wounds." Keep in mind that this is only if you're moving forward at a steady pace with one another.

During each chapter, you need to be evaluating your specific situation. You may feel as if the relationship has reached its end. This is obviously not ideal, but perfectly fine. Read on to Chapter 9 if you need to now understand what comes next.

But if things are going swimmingly, then this was a pretty fun chapter for you. You reconnected! In Chapter 7, we'll dive in to the best ways to bring up and resolve your issues. Then, you can move on to being the happy, wonderful couple you've been wanting all this time.

# Chapter 6 Take Aways

**Key Points:**

★ Make sure you're ready for an in-person meeting. The last thing you want to do is reach out to your ex and come across as bitter, desperate or needy.

★ Every couple's separation time period is different, but we would suggest at least 1-3 months of distance before attempting to call.

★ Remember, you are in control of this situation. Leverage the psychological strategies in this chapter to be as prepared as possible.

★ Recap of the 6 Steps:

    ★ Step 1: The Call - Calling your ex for a meeting might be intimidating. But stay strong, there's a 99% chance you'll get a YES on your invitation.

    ★ Step 2: Prepare for the Date - Once you get a date, remember this is the first step on the journey to a full reconciliation. Make sure you're looking good and feeling good so as to appear as confident as you can be.

★ Step 3: The Flashback Maneuver - This is an extremely powerful technique that will instantly send them a signal to remind them of all the good times you've had together.

★ Step 4: Ending the Date - Bow out when things are going really well as you want to end the date on a high note. This leaves them wanting more, which is exactly where you want to be.

★ Step 5: The 2nd, 3rd, and 4th+ Dates - It's good to have a little fun and break out of your shell. But not too much - you still want to appear mysterious.

★ Step 6: Make it More - It's time to figure out where you two stand. We'll discuss in Chapter 7 how to heal old wounds and make your relationship official.

## Action Steps:

- ☐ Complete each of the steps as outlined in the chapter:
    - ☐ Step 1: The Call
    - ☐ Step 2: Prepare for the Date
    - ☐ Step 3: The Flashback Maneuver
    - ☐ Step 4: Ending the Date
    - ☐ Step 5: The 2nd, 3rd, and 4th+ Dates
    - ☐ Step 6: Make it more

## 7

# Heal The Wounds - On Both Ends

Sometimes, as we mentioned in Chapter 1, couples break up for little reasons or maybe over general life stress. Other times there was a major reason for the break-up – cheating, lying, lack of trust, anger issues, etc. And chances are, while you and your ex have had some good, light fun on your first couple of reconciliation dates, your ex will not move forward with you until those issues are resolved.

Let's tackle that, shall we?

This is by far one of the most difficult aspects of reconciliation. How do you get past lingering arguments or disagreements? There may be a few apologies unspoken or feelings left hurt. Keep in mind while we discuss this that you need to be open and humble with your ex. If you really truly love them and want this to work, you have to be willing to compromise or even just let it go.

## How To Move Past *Your* Mistakes

After the 3rd or 4th date with your ex, "the big issue" was most likely brought up. First, you listen. Intently! Let them speak their peace. This doesn't mean you can't be honest about your potentially differing opinion, it just means that you speak with love. Share with them why you feel the way you do, while putting yourself "out there."

Stay away from "I promise I can change" or "Give me another chance." This almost sets you up for failure. The truth is, we are all human and we *will* make mistakes. The difference is how we choose to handle them.

Still wondering how to apply this to your specific situation? Take a look at the **READ** Technique below.

This is a surefire way to show your ex you're mature enough for a reconciliation.

**R**ecognize the issue

**E**xplain that you're aware it was a problem in your relationship

**A**pologize – with meaning

**D**escribe how you'll work hard to be the best partner you can be

For example, "I know you're right. I do have a problem with jealousy. And I've been working hard to relieve myself of that issue. I'm very sorry for the pain I caused you. I hope you know, though, that it's because I love you so much that I fell into that trap. I will work hard every day to make sure I do the right thing for both of us."

## Overcoming Trust Issues

***What happens if ? ---> my ex doesn't trust me anymore.***
It's not the best situation to be in. But you *can* re-gain their trust. It's just going to take some time and perseverance. You must must MUST be patient. Let them slowly get to know the "new" you. An appropriate amount of time to ease into things is

about 2-3 months of light dating (depending upon what happened). If they're still withholding, you need to lovingly tell them you are in this for them. But if they cannot forgive you and move on in a legitimate amount of time, then we doubt they ever will.

***What happens if? ---> my infidelity led to our break-up.***
This is an extreme case of loss of trust. See, while your ex is enjoying seeing you come to them for forgiveness on bended knee, the thought of you cheating again is understandably creeping around in the back of their head. Unless they are willing to accept your apology and healthily forget about your infidelity, this can cause serious problems down the road. And you need to make sure you are trustworthy and making them feel safe. A person's heart is a sacred thing, don't mess around with them if you aren't really committed this time.

## How To Move Past *Their* Mistakes

You're finding it hard to forgive. We got you. We know it's not the easiest thing in the world. Especially if it's something you have to keep forgiving them for. Learning how to forgive someone is such a vital technique to nail down for not only this relationship – but in all your relationships. Take a look at the steps below to get a better grasp on how to forgive your ex before it ruins your chances of reconciliation.

1) Pinpoint exactly what it is you need to forgive. Be able to articulate it to your ex.

2) How does it make you feel? Betrayed? Irritated? If you're meant to be with you ex, they will care about your feelings and want to hear you out.

3) Tell them everything. You need to clearly state what you uncovered in #1 & 2. Use phrases like "I felt very hurt when…" They can't deny how their actions made you feel.

4) Listen to what they have to say – maybe there is a reason why they acted out. This will tell you a lot about their maturity level. If they're able to accept your words and wholeheartedly apologize, then you've got a winner on your hands.

5) Forgive them – if you can. Hopefully by this step you will feel affirmed and rejuvenated just by letting it all out.

6) Let it go. Do not bring this up in any future arguments or discussions.

---

*A note from Kimberly:*

*Compared to Ryan, I felt a lot more pain as a result of our split because, well, I'm a woman! After a couple of weeks passed I thought… "How in the world is he living without me?" and that hurt. After we got back together, Ryan made it clear to me that he hated being apart and was sorry that I ever felt sad. Let me tell you – it was hard work to move past that and trust that we would be together forever. It was something I very much struggled with. But I knew how important it was for him to know I trust him.*

---

What you need to work on, now, is not bringing up old fights every time something not-so-great happens. This can KILL your relationship for good. Once you've practiced the forgiveness techniques above, you gotta let it go. But it's important to note that while you can "let things go," you will *not* overlook it if it happens again. It's at that point that you need to re-evaluate their sincerity and perhaps move on.

## It's Time To Seal the Deal

Okay, we've worked through just about everything that may come up in your steps toward reconciliation. Now, it's time to ask... where do you stand? This can be quite simple. This conversation should come up naturally, especially if you two have worked through any lingering issues as we discussed in this chapter.

Of course, the best time to bring it up is when you're both feeling good – maybe after a great dinner date or fun night out with friends. Prepare to feel a bit vulnerable. Since you're the one who originally sought out the reconciliation, the answer to this question will tell you whether or not their heart is in it as much as yours. This is key!

So here it is... *"I feel like things have been going great for us. I'm so glad to have had the chance to see you again, and work through some of the issues we've had. I want to be with you. Do you want to get back together?"*

And then wait for the response. We know, that is the hard part sometimes. But the reward can be great. If your ex responds positively, then

**CONGRATULATIONS!!** We are truly thrilled for you. In the next chapter we'll discuss how to keep your love fresh and avoid arguments in the future.

If your ex hesitates or flat-out says "No," then it's time to take a big step back. Depending upon your particular situation (perhaps if they're still having trouble forgiving you), then you can certainly back off and try again in a few weeks or so. You'll know when it's time to stop altogether. It's a tough realization, but again, we don't want you to waste your time. Skip forward to Chapter 9 as we walk through the next step.

# Chapter 7 Take Aways

**Key Points:**

★ Chances are, your ex will want to re-visit old wounds and arguments before agreeing to get back together with you. After a few fun dates, you're ready to tackle those issues.

★ Be open, humble and honest with your ex during this discussion.

★ Stay away from statements like "I promise I can change," as this just sets you up for failure.

★ If you need to do some apologizing, implement the READ Technique to move past lingering arguments.

★ A loss of trust or infidelity requires extreme patience on your end. You need to be understanding of the time they may need to forgive you and move past it.

★ If you need to do some forgiving, it's important to first be open and honest about why they hurt you and how they need to change.

★ Once the issues have been resolved, do NOT bring up old fights as this can kill your relationship for good. You both have to be able to move past your issues.

★ Seal the deal! If things are going well, it's time to ask your ex if they'd like to get back together. Wait patiently for their response.

**Action Steps:**

☐ Scroll back to Chapter 1 to re-visit the issues that caused your break-up.

☐ If necessary, implement the READ Technique to apologize for anything you may have done to hurt them.

☐ If necessary, review the 6 steps of forgiveness to make sure you can fully move past anything they may have done to hurt you.

# 8

# How To Keep Things Hot!

Congratulations on your How To Get Your Ex Back, friend! We are so very happy for you. We trust you will continue on with a happy and healthy relationship. But, you aren't done yet! Haven't you always heard that relationships take work? You don't want to make the same mistakes you did the first time around.

In this chapter, we'll go through the best ways to keep your love life fun while avoiding future problems with your now-partner.

## Don't Smother

When you've finally reached the point of reconciliation, there is a great temptation to spend every waking moment with them. Steer clear from that. You want them to know that while you are over the moon for them, you've still got other things going on. Support each other in your independence.

*A note from Kimberly:*

*I remember the feeling the next morning after Ryan asked me to be his girlfriend again. I could barely stand still! But I fought all urges to call, text or make plans. He completely pursued me, even though we were already back together. Just barely a week later, he flew to meet me while I was on vacation to surprise me for Christmas! Needless to say, it was a fun time.*

## Keep Bettering Yourself

Just because you're back together with your ex does not mean you should stop working on yourself. Continue the good routines of healthy eating and exercising, spending time with friends, and trying new things.

## Accept Changes in Each Other

If you two were apart for a longer period of time, there may be some changes in them (and you!) that may take some getting used to. For example, you've been exercising, right?! It may be hard to keep up with that cardio routine now that they're back in your life. Well, how about including them in your weekly workouts?

They may have a new friend that you've never met. Be open to it! Invite the friend out to dinner with the three of you so the new friend can get to know you. Maybe they even have a new job… it's good to know that both of you were moving forward with your lives instead of moping around. Spend some time getting re-acquainted. It won't take long.

*A note from Ryan:*

*Kimberly had a lot going on in her "new" life. She moved, got a new job, and made a lot of friends I had never met. I was thrilled for her. But having known her upside-down and inside-out for the 3 years we had been dating, it was definitely an adjustment. I wanted to know her again, so I eased my way back into her life while letting her keep on with her routines.*

## Make it FUN!

Remember back in Chapter 1 when we discussed reasons for your break-up? One of them included getting stuck in a stale routine with your partner of boring nights and sluggish appearances. Let's not do that again, okay? It's one thing to be comfortable with them and have a loungy movie night. But it's another thing to make that your whole life!

It's time to amp up your love life with a few tips & tricks. You should never stop romancing your partner. NEVER! You both need to make a conscious effort to keep the romance alive and well. This does wonders for the overall health of your relationship. Some women are tempted to think that it's only the guy's job to plan getaways or write a sweet love note. NOPE! This goes for both men & women.

Follow our guide below to get some ideas:

- Daily reminders: There are a lot of ways to remind your partner how much you care. Be creative and consistent!

- Wake up like each day is a new day. The "I Love You" you said last night won't cut it for the week. Tell them often that you love them and even more importantly – tell them why.

- Leave a note in their car

- Have their favorite meal waiting for them when they get home

- Surprise them at work with a lunch date

- Send them an email detailing your favorite night with them

- Date nights! We urge you to keep up with your date nights. It's so important to make this part of your weekly schedule.

- The "go-to"… dinner and a movie

- Spa treatments – his and hers massages!
- Ice skating / roller blading
- Long walks
- Beach day – get some beach cruisers and enjoy some sun & exercise
- Theme parks
- Go see a play or musical
- Game nights
- Wine tasting
- Sporting events
- Picnic at the park
- Weekend getaways
- Athletic competition - sports, triathlons, etc.
- Bowling
- Mini-golf
- …And much more. Try new things! Make it an adventure!

**Quality time is a must!**
Staring at each other across the dinner table at night is not quality time. We mean actually talking with each other and sharing what's been on your heart.

- If you've been working a bunch, tell your love how much you miss them and plan a date to catch up.

- End-of-day cuddles and kisses are the best. Hold each other close and tell each other about your day.

## Stay Honeymooners!

- Don't ever forget the feeling of losing your partner and getting them back. That feeling alone can make you rush home and hold them in your arms all night.

- Be affectionate! Frequent kisses, hugs or a sweet pinch on the booty can help keep the romance alive. If you lose this aspect of your relationship, you will no doubt start to feel distant.

- Feel yourself falling in a rut? It's time to get out and do something. Remember the tips above – you gotta keep the romance alive!

## How to Avoid Disagreements in the Future

Let's say things are moving along nicely. But you're afraid to disagree with them for fear of rocking the boat again. Look, disagreements are fine! And healthy! You're not going to go your whole life in a state of blissful peace. There *will* be instances in which you're not exactly in line with your partner. Below are some ways to avoid big, dramatic fights.

~ Keep your cool. Don't flip out and raise your voice.

~ Don't misplace your anger or frustration. If you had a bad day at work, don't take it out on your partner.

~ Don't let an argument linger. It's important to get it resolved before it blows up into an even bigger fight.

~ Use key words like "I feel," or "that makes me feel"… this way, your partner will see that you aren't simply being stubborn, you are actually feeling hurt.

~ Don't bring up the past. Although tempting, you'll remember how we

warned about that. It can only do you
wrong.

~ Avoid flare-ups over small issues. Pick
your battles.

~ Do not, under any circumstance, let
your anger get the best of you and say
something you don't mean. Even
though it wasn't true, your words
cannot be taken back. This could really
hurt the future of your relationship.

**What happens if ? ---> my now-boy/girlfriend is asking if I
dated while we were apart.**
This topic is bound to come up. You and your ex may
be on a "don't ask, don't tell" policy about dates/
lovers you had when you were broken up. Honestly,
that's the best way to avoid any hurt feelings or
jealousy. Trust us on that one. But make sure to be up
front about any sexual partners you may have had.
They deserve to know those details if they're going
to be intimate with you again.

If your ex insists on knowing everyone you dated and
what you did, it's up to you how much you want to
release. Tell them the truth, but maybe tone it down

a notch. Instead of "We kissed passionately as the rain poured down on us," try "We kissed." You'll know what feels right.

### *What happens if ? ---> my family/friends don't agree with us getting back together.*

Opinions of your friends and family are hard to shut out. Give them a break, they're only doing it because they love you. But, it is important to remember that while they are key people in your life, they do not run your life. It is okay to let them know you prefer for them to not get involved with your dating life.

If these are people that you see on an everyday basis, it's okay to give them an update and tell them how happy you are. Ask them to please accept your decision and treat you and your partner with respect. Hopefully they're able to do so! Don't let a nagging mom or best friend get in the way of your relationship bliss.

# Chapter 8 Take Aways

## Key Points:

★     Just because you're back together with your ex does not mean it's time to get lazy. Often times when couples reunite they fall into the same old (and boring) routines and stop working on bettering themselves. Continue with the positive attitude, healthy eating and exercising.

★     Be sure not to smother your ex when you first get back together. You need to let them have their independence and make sure to keep yours.

★     In order to keep your relationship HOT, you've got to have fun dates and do romantic things.

★     Disagreements are fine and healthy, so make sure to use techniques that will keep those fights from becoming too nasty.

★     Be honest with your ex about things you may have done while broken up, but be sure to leave those memories in the past right after.

★ If "key" people in your life disagree with your relationship, it's important to remember that while you love and respect them, they do not run your life.

## Action Steps:

☐ Continue working to better yourself. This means staying in touch with a positive mindset, eating healthily and working out on a consistent basis. You'll want to stay your best for your partner!

☐ Plan a fun date night at least once a week.

☐ It's all in the little things: Do romantic gestures as often as possible to remind your partner how much you care.

# Relationship Checkpoint

If you've made it this far and everything is smooth sailing, that means you're back together with your ex. We're truly thrilled for you and wish you all the best in the future. Thank you for trusting us in this process and sticking it out to the very end.

## CONGRATULATIONS!

**However...**

If things have not been going good at all, it may be time to move on. Not every relationship has a happy ending, and you know what? THAT'S OKAY. We've got a bit more to discuss so please read on to Chapter 9. Don't worry - we've got you covered.

# 9

# When It's Time To Say Goodbye

Now's the time to really be honest with yourself. You know when things aren't right. It's just a matter of if you're willing to admit that and move on with your life. It can be a scary thing, so it's understandable that you might be having trouble closing the book on this particular relationship.

You may have known all along that your ex was toxic for you, or you could've only just realized it as you tried to reconcile. Regardless, it's time. Time to get on to a better life! And we'll help you do it.

## Make a Complete Break From Your Ex

It may tempting to call, text or "casually" run into your ex. Sure, you might miss them at first. But this is not okay. This will only serve to make you look desperate and incapable of being independent. Not only that, but it only renews the pain and hurt feelings each time you talk to or see them! You want to make a complete break. If that means deleting them off your phone, AIM, Facebook, etc., then we suggest you do that.

You'll never forget your ex. And that's fine! Remember the good parts and learn from the mistakes you made. While you'll want to pin all the problems on your ex, chances are there were some things you could stand to improve on. Take some time to figure out what those things are so you can be aware of them for future relationships.

## Grieve Responsibly

The worst thing you can do right now is to pretend like nothing's wrong. Trying to skate past the grieving process can be dangerous! Bottled-up feelings can come back to haunt you in future relationships, and we don't want that.

It's healthy to mourn when a big break-up occurs. They say you'll experience the 5 Stages of Grief: Denial, anger, bargaining, depression and finally, acceptance. Be aware of this as you heal so as not to become a victim of your pain. It's also not wise to make HUGE life decisions during this time. You don't want to make a bad situation worse by making a rash decision motivated by your grief.

So, how do you get past this?

## Build On the Positive

We're sure you agree that the health tips and attitude tricks we've discussed have really done great things for you. Well, okay then... keep 'em up! The best way to get past this is to keep moving. Even if your relationship didn't work out as first desired, you can now head into this new season of your life with a great outlook and a healthy mind, body and soul.

**Continue Dating!**
We can understand that the sometimes the last thing you feel like doing is going on a date. Getting into

another relationship may not be high on your priority list right now, but dating should be. It's an important routine to keep up! Remember our go-to method? "Just Say Yes!"

Date casually until you find a connection. Take a step back and decide if you are ready to get serious with someone again before you make a commitment. You'll want to avoid rebound relationships since they can only stand to hurt you more.

**Appreciate The Good**
Sometimes when we're knee-deep in a troublesome relationship, we overlook the great blessings we have. Take a look around you – what are you thankful for? Do some self-reflection about your current situation. Here are some ways to divert attention away from your break-up and onto your future:

- Do for others – volunteering will keep you busy and help you give back
- Spend more time with your family
- Plan fun things to do with your friends
- Travel
- Check some things off your bucket list

~ Focus on your career

## Be Patient – Time Will Heal You

It may seem like your life is over. We can assure you, it is not. Of course you'll feel pain, but it *will* get better. Maybe this has happened to you before, so you know you're capable of picking up the pieces and moving on. Doesn't mean it will hurt any less, but alas you'll be just fine. Better, even!

See, every experience we go through ends up making us stronger in the end; mainly because we learn from them. Perhaps you learned not to choose a mate similar to your ex because of a difference in personality, interests or religion.

## A Better You

You may not know it yet, but you'll be grateful for this relationship one day. You'll be grateful for the fun memories you shared and the things you learned from it. We're so confident that if you follow the guidelines we've shared, you'll be happy with the results.

Remember, this is not going to happen overnight. Handle yourself responsibly and with grace as you move forward to a healthier, happier life.

# Chapter 9 Take Aways

## Key Points:

★ Remember, your life is not OVER. You will move on and you will be happy.

★ Once you know that your relationship has ended, it's imperative that you cease all communication with your ex. You don't want to re-live the pain and hurt feelings more than you have to.

★ You'll never forget your ex, and that's okay. Remember the good memories and learn from your mistakes.

★ It's okay to grieve, but don't let this get in the way of YOU. Your life without your ex may be just beginning, but you have an incredible future ahead of you with limitless possibilities.

★ Keep up with your dating regimen. While your heart may not be ready for Mr. Right just yet, you'll get there and dating will help you do so.

★ Each experience we go through ends up making us stronger in the end.

**Action Steps:**

☐   Implement a permanent BLACKLIST of all things having to do with your ex. You won't be able to move on properly unless you delete all pictures off Facebook, remove framed photos from your house, stow away old love letters, etc. Do not contact your ex in any way.

☐   Continue using your online dating profiles as a way to meet potential dates.

☐   Try to keep your mind off your grief by doing for others, spending more time with your family, traveling, focusing on your career or crossing off fun things on your bucket list.

☐   To put everything in the past, write down how you're feeling at this exact moment in your journal. One day, you'll re-open that journal and see how much you've grown.